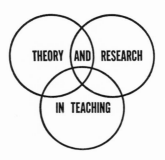

Teachers College, Columbia University
Arno A. Bellack, editor

Recent years have witnessed a resurgence of interest on the part of educational researchers in the teaching process. Volumes in the *Theory and Research in Teaching* series report significant studies of instructional procedures in a variety of educational settings, at various organizational levels in the schools, and in many of the subjects included in the curriculum. These studies present fresh perspectives on teaching both to educational researchers and to practitioners in the schools.

Maurice Gibbons

Simon Fraser University

INDIVIDUALIZED INSTRUCTION
A DESCRIPTIVE ANALYSIS

TEACHERS COLLEGE PRESS

Teachers College   Columbia University

New York, New York

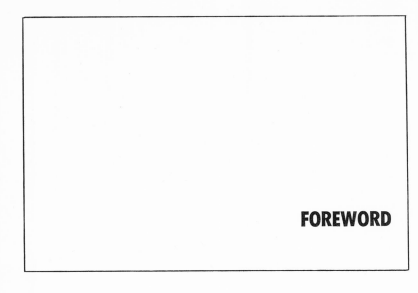

FOREWORD

The contemporary movement toward individualized instruction in the schools has gained the enthusiastic support of many educationists and laymen throughout the country. Numerous proposals for individualized programs are set forth in professional and popular journals, and many schools report efforts to establish such programs. But, as Dr. Gibbons observes, the notion of individualized instruction remains notoriously vague, and the current interest in individualization has taken a bewildering array of forms. In this monograph Dr. Gibbons performs a useful service in analyzing the concept of individualization, proposing a taxonomy for classifying the many varieties of individualized programs, and constructing an observational instrument for profiling the major curricular features of individualized programs in the schools. He demonstrates the utility of the instrument by using it to describe ten individualized programs that have been developed in the United States and in Great Britain.

Teachers, administrators, and laymen will find Dr. Gibbons' analysis an invaluable resource in their attempts to understand the movement toward individualization of instruction.

Arno A. Bellack

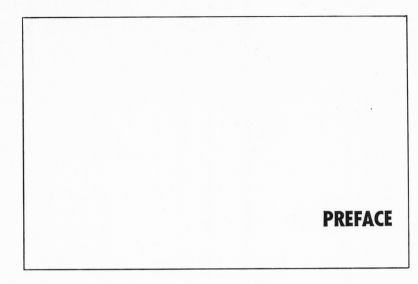

PREFACE

The term *individualized* has a humanistic ring to it that immediately catches the ear of anyone disenchanted with the factory din of regular schooling. To me it suggested a specific instructional procedure adapted to the learning style and personality of each student. But even preliminary reading on the subject and visits to a few lighthouse schools made it clear that the term is used for many different kinds of instructional procedures, that few of them—very few of them—involve a marked degree of adaptation to individual students, and that fewer still have demonstrated significant effects on the achievement or the lives of students.

Before designing and launching my own individualized program—an attempt to establish an experimental open classroom in a traditional high school—I attempted to find some order in the array of programs and to find out what an individualized program really is. This book is the result of that endeavor.

I received a great deal of help in the process. David Purpel and Peter Neumeyer of the Harvard Graduate School of Education made it possible for me to conduct my work in my own way and provided guidance when it was most needed. My colleague, R. Gordon MacIntosh of The University of Alberta, discussed the problems of analysis with me at length and made several suggestions that are incorporated in this work. The Xerox Corporation provided the scholarship that made it possible to eat while I wrote. My wife, Marian, typed the several drafts and my children, Karen and Geoff, helped me with the proofreading.

I thank them all.

Maurice Gibbons

Burnaby, British Columbia
March 1971

CONTENTS

INDIVIDUALIZED INSTRUCTION

ONE

THE PROFUSION OF
INDIVIDUALIZED PROGRAMS

The formal development of individualized instructional programs in America began in the later decades of the nineteenth century as a reaction against the age-graded, lock-step system in which all students, regardless of differences among them, were constrained to study the same materials in the same way for the same length of time (Harris, 1960, p. 222). Although the main current of educational practice has continued resolutely in the traditional channels of the graded system, fixed in its course by the textbook and examinations, an increasing number of programs that make schooling more adaptable to differences among students have been proposed and developed (De Haan and Doll, 1964, p. 10; Shane, 1962, p. 44). Arguments for breaking down uniformity of instruction gained support with the appearance of instruments for measuring human abilities shortly after the turn of the century. With the increasing sophistication of psychometric tools it has become clear that students differ not

1

only in intelligence but in creativity (Wallach and Kogan, 1965) and in at least eighty elements of intellect (Guilford, 1967, p. 65). It also became clear that great differences between competence and performance are possible, and that inequalities in intellect, physical ability, and social behavior, great in childhood, increase as students move through the grades (Thomas and Thomas, 1965, p. 3). It has been dramatically shown that among eighty ninth graders, readings and mathematics test scores ranged from grades three and four to college sophomore and junior levels (pp. 30–33)—yet graded mass teaching continues.

Many of the proposals for changing the traditional system are referred to as individualized programs, others exhibit the unmistakable hallmarks of individualization even though they do not bear the title, and to these may be added still others, programs not necessarily associated with the school but obviously individualized: tutorials, correspondence courses, and the informal programs of independent study any man embarks upon when he seriously asks a question and pursues the answer by observing, opening a book, or talking to one who may know. Together such programs constitute a widely diverse family. They are based on different interpretations of individualization. They are inspired by different philosophies and theories, influenced by different technologies and expertise, and confounded by the ambiguity of their label. In fact, the term *individualized instructional program* is used to describe such a varied assortment of curricula that it is no longer a useful, restrictive category of instructional methods. It likely never was.

A brief list of these programs, even one that excludes pre–nineteenth-century forms and those proposed for such specific subject areas as reading (references concerned with individualization of particular subjects and levels are listed in Parker, 1963, and Spitzer, 1968), clearly indicates that individualized programs have been part of American formal schooling almost from its inception, and that the revived interest in individualization has taken a bewildering array of forms.

Types of Programs

Tutoring. The original individual instruction program, tutoring was once exclusively for the rich; at least one writer has suggested it can be employed in contemporary public schools (Polos, 1966).

Correspondence Courses. One of the first efforts to individualize instruction, correspondence courses were available as early as 1873. By 1882 a systematic plan for the study of foreign languages was announced. Weekly assignments of reading and translating sent to the student were corrected by the teacher "with notes and suggestions adapted to his individual needs" (Noffsinger, 1926, p. 10). A recent Carnegie Corporation Study showed that between 3.5 and 5 million students were enrolled in correspondence courses (Pearse, 1967, p. 10).

Self-Paced Unit Plans. By 1888 Preston Search had initiated the Pueblo Plan, a laboratory scheme permitting a student to pace his own coverage of the course rather than await his turn in daily recitation (Search, 1894). Parkhurst's Dalton Laboratory Plan (1922) and Carleton Washburne's Winnetka Plan (1963), both influenced by Frederick Burk, former President of San Francisco State Normal School, presented course work in self-instructional units that each student worked through as fast as he could. In the Winnetka Plan "common essentials" studied in these intensive units each morning were separated from free, group, and creative activities students could choose each afternoon. The Project for Individually Prescribed Instruction at Pittsburgh (The Oakleaf Project) and such independent study programs as the one at Nova High School (Kohn, 1967, p. 31), also feature self-paced unit-sheet packages and individual assistance. In Project PLAN—Program for Learning in Accordance with Needs—the instructional materials are organized into modules of approximately five specific objectives and the materials required to achieve each of them (Flanagan, 1970).

Programmed and Computorized Instruction. Programmed teaching by text and machine is "an attempt to obtain the kind of behavioral control shown possible in the laboratory" (Holland, 1960, p. 275). Each segment of the course is divided into "small but rigorous steps, each of which is rewarding" (Skinner, 1961, p. 3). The program may be adapted to the individual by altering the method and sequence of presenting these units. The student works at his own pace and either corrects his answer to the question in each frame or has it corrected for him automatically. In *intrinsic* programs incorrect answers may result in the presentation of first or second order *branches* leading to a correctional sequence or a sub-program (Crowder, 1963, p. 85). The *adaptive* teaching machine gives or withdraws assistance and changes the difficulty of the material according to a running computation of the student's performance (Glaser, 1965, p. 232). SOCRATES and PLATO are multi-media adaptive systems that combine a responsive typewriter or digital device, tapes, films, slides, and other audio-visual aides with programs. The system presents material on the basis of a pre-instruction rating and the student's performance on the program (pp. 162–207). Other forms, as for instance

Omar K. Moore's responsive environment laboratory, permit students freedom in exploring the possibilities of the equipment.

Independent Study Programs. The fashion of the sixties in individualized instruction, independent study refers to any program that for some portion of the school day is "characterized by the attainment of some freedom from the constraint of supervision" (Bishop, 1967, p. 9). There seems to be little agreement on a more detailed definition, although "two major elements—individual study (study by one's self) and self-directed study (study independent from a regularly structured curricula)—appear frequently in association with the term" (Cyphert, 1967, p. 206). Many schools have been influenced by the recommendation in the Trump Plan (Trump and Bayman, 1961) that courses should include independent study along with lectures, seminars, and individual consultation, but they often adopt independent study on a token basis, involving only a few students for a small portion of the school week for activities indistinguishable from familiar homework, project, and research assignments. Alexander and Hines (1967) eliminate these pseudo-forms in their definition and classification. They define independent study as activity in secondary schools that is "somewhat independent" of class, organization, and practice, in which teachers and other professionals are primarily resources for the student who pursues his own aims for values intrinsic in the work (p. 12). Their classification suggests the range still possible: independent study as an option, individually guided independent study, job-oriented independent study, independent study seminars (students share their work and findings) and "Quest-type" programs for the development of special aptitudes (students work on personal projects, con-

sulting with an advisor). Within these categories there is
still great variation among particular programs in the per
cent of the student population involved, the portion of
the school day made available, the kinds of curriculum
decisions the students can make, and the degree to which
independent study is independent of course require-
ments. The Montessori Method (1964), recently revived
in America (Rambusch, 1962), is a form of independent
study offering the student a range of alternative activities
he can explore according to his interests; the teacher is
available if needed to assist him in working through the
sets of learning materials he chooses.

Grouping for Individualization. Sub-grouping for
teaching (ability groups, interest and activity groups,
teachability groups) and group work as a method (T-
groups, non-directive group teaching, sensitivity group
work) have both been suggested as means of individualizing instruction, the first by reducing the differences
among students, the second by encouraging development
through controlled social interaction. Some advocates
claim rather paradoxically that grouping is a necessary
part of individualization (Clymer and Kearney, 1962,
p. 268), in part because the individual supposedly gives
personal relevance to experiences he shares with the other
members of the group (DeHaan and Doll, 1964, p. 13).
But there is strong opposition to the idea that teaching
becomes more personalized in groups. Parker (1963, p.
110), for instance, claims that ability grouping is likely
to freeze instruction at a single level on the assumption
that the level of the group has been determined. Others
argue that no matter how closely diagnosed, any group
organized for homogeneity on one dimension will vary
widely in many other characteristics (e.g., Harris, 1960,
pp. 223–224). As Westby-Gibson (1966, pp. 10–11) points

out, study after study has concluded that grouping by whatever criteria seldom reduces variability by more than 20 per cent. "Groups cannot be homogeneous because individuals are not homogeneous within themselves." Carl Rogers (1951, 1961) has promulgated student-centered teaching on the principles of client-centered therapy; Herbert Thelen (1963) has proposed a method based on group dynamics, in which teacher and pupils plan the program together to organize "reality-based" investigations with opportunities for personal inquiry. T-groups and sensitivity groups have been introduced into the classroom experimentally, but are more often employed in teacher training.

Administrative Plans. Most innovations for individualization require modifications of classroom and school procedures, but many plans for school organization and operation have also been introduced to make individualization possible. There are numerous plans for removing the age-grade barrier, permitting students to advance through the levels of schooling at more individual rates (e.g., "continuous promotion," "continuous progress," "acceleration," "dual progress," "advanced placement," the non-graded school, Leicestershire's "families" of students, and so on). And there are numerous plans for dividing students into classes according to their intelligence, ability, or achievement. Harold G. Shane (1962, p. 49) lists thirty-five such plans: "x, y, z classes," "homogeneous streaming," "tracking," and the like. Other plans introduce alternatives for students in the form of electives. Between 1900 and 1930 the courses offered in all subject areas of four-year high schools increased from 50 to 306, a trend that has continued (Harris, 1960, pp. 1263–1264). Team teaching was introduced, in part, to free teachers for small groups and individual consulta-

tion by having one teacher lecture to several classes at
once. The use of para-professionals is recommended in
the Diederich, Rutgers, and Trump plans, but little sustained individualization is likely to be achieved by
reorganization that does not include lowering the teacher-
student ratio and changing instructional methods.
Kapfer's (1968) management strategy is a systematic
procedure for organizing a variety of individualized instructional techniques.

   Personal Programs. These forms of individualization are
usually found in private schools, where the institution can
be adapted to the child rather than the child to the institutional pattern of prescribed instruction and competitive
achievement (Neill, 1960, p. 4). Although they owe much
of their philosophy and strategy to the progressive movement, these programs are more inspired by such work as
Summerhill (Neill, 1960), *The Vanishing Adolescent*
(Friedenberg, 1959), *Growing up Absurd* and *Compulsory Mis-education* (Goodman, 1956, 1966), *How Children Fail* and *How Children Learn* (Holt, 1964, 1967)
and *Childhood and Society* (Erikson, 1964), rather than
by Dewey and Kilpatrick. At Summerhill, the exemplar
and prototype, and at such offshoots as The Everdale
Place in Ontario, the emphasis is on freedom for healthy
psychosocial growth, not just self-directed study, but self
actualization. Students take part in all decisions concern-
ing themselves, rules are minimized, and students attend
only those classes they wish to. They combine community
in their "town meetings" with solitude or informal group
play during the plentiful free time after classes on the
traditional pattern are over.

   Remediation and Teaching Exceptional Children.
More progress has been achieved in the clinical diagnosis
and specific treatment of individual learning problems—

whether the cause lies in very high or low mental endowment, damaging school experience, physical or mental impairment, or psycho-social problems—than in any other form of individualized instruction. The teamwork of neurologists, psychiatrists, clinical psychologists, technicians, teachers, and counsellors in attacking problems in special education is a model for development in all individual instruction. As Edgar Doll (1965, p. 11) points out, "Each of us is a slow learner in some area at some speed and for some reasons." Lawrence J. Peter, among others, has already broken this ground with his book on *Prescriptive Teaching* (1965), which describes a method for the adaptation of teaching and resources to individuals based on diagnosis of their needs within regular school contexts. Hilda Taba (1962) recommends a grosser form in which intensive diagnosis is the basis for determining curriculum units for a class.

Miscellaneous Individualized Programs and Suggestions. Many recommendations for individualization are dangerously trivial, distracting attention from the need for major changes and encouraging teachers to claim to be individualizing while continuing mass teaching methods. For instance, the 1964 yearbook of the Association for Supervision and Curriculum Development offers such suggestions as "observing and listening to learners with increased care and concern" and "becoming more sensitive to clues which indicates how teachers can help" (Doll, 1964, p. 160). But there are many others who make suggestions for far-reaching change. For instance, Goodman (1966, pp. 33–34) urges that students be permitted to travel and to work on farms as part of their formal schooling, and Newmann and Oliver (1967, pp. 36–37) suggest, as part of their proposal to involve students in the adult community and in tasks that take them outside schools, that students and adults meet in seminars to examine "the broadest questions raised in planning for education in community." The Outward Bound Program (*Outward Bound Schools* [n.d.], pp. 4–5) now operating in at least four American states during the summer, with its culmination in a three-day "solo" in wilderness survival, presents a challenge to individual courage and stamina that could be a valuable addition to paler formal schooling. One of the most radical developments in individualization is occurring at the preschool level, where specialists are tutoring infants and training mothers to tutor their own by stimulating the child with objects, toys, games, and tasks appropriate for his stage of physical and mental development (Hess and Bear, 1968; Pines, 1967), making certain that experience and environment facilitate the fullest realization of potentialities at each level of maturation.

This list is still far from complete, but it is long enough to illustrate the confusion about individualized and other instruction that confounds understanding, and the fragmentation of effort that defeats attempts to develop markedly different and better forms of schooling. The list is long enough to suggest our preoccupation with partial solutions, fashionable modifications, and one-shot innovations that can be introduced without seriously disturbing traditional relationships and procedures in the schools. And although the list is long on ideas, it is short on ideas with demonstrated values. Few of the programs have been developed through controlled stages of refinement to a polished state and few, if any, can be recommended on the grounds of proven, desirable increments in student accomplishment. The goal implicit in the programs on this list seems to be the provision of separate, uniquely appropriate education for each student. But each program falls short of this implicit idea, and worse, is often designed to progress no further than practices arrived at through considerable adjustment to apparent constraints in existing school environments, organization, resources, staff, and curriculum. It is as if each group—administrator-planners, programmed-learning specialists, publishers, group-dynamics theorists, curriculum developers, researchers, and so on—were working toward a vision of general education quite different from the others. That is, in the universe of schooling, the galaxies of specialists seem to be rushing away from each other and from the synthesis that education in general and individualized instruction in particular desperately need.

Synthesis

What kind of synthesis is needed? Certainly the additive approach to school change—introducing television, study packages, teaching teams, small group discussion, independent study, and so on—is a slow method and has illustrated time and again that the accretion of bright new approaches to the old stones of schooling does not a new institution make. Schooling must be regularly re-invented whole—or close to it. Re-invention can best be accomplished by a coming together of specialists and practitioners from a variety of fields working on a common problem under a minimum of constraints, but operating within the structure of a regular school district. In such an environment—a clinical school or center for educational development—teachers can be trained or retrained for new roles and for the dissemination of the new form of schooling. Training teachers for new roles in such centers would break the cycle of training for teaching in traditional systems that is a major obstacle to both the evolution and revolution of public school education now based on the tell-practice-test model.

Procedures

Whether a change in education is shaped in such a clinical center or in a regular school, whether it involves some form of individualized instruction, five important and separate sets of procedures should be followed to increase the likelihood that the synthesis will be conceptually thorough and that new forms will reach maturity in development.

Analysis. Analysis comprises the *collection* of theories, practices, and research data relevant to the form of schooling under examination; the *organization* of this information into forms that facilitate study and comparison; and the *isolation* of common terms, elements, principles, and problems. Its basic purpose is the utilization of what is known and what has already been done to focus on what needs to be done.

Formulation. Formulation comprises the *invention* of a way of doing "what needs to be done" by the team of specialists and practitioners, the *elaboration* of the invention into a conceptual model of school practice, and the theoretical *testing and modification* of the model by the team and others. Its basic purpose is the creation and refinement of a model that has the greatest apparent potential for achieving the stated educational puroposes of the team.

Development. Development involves the *translation* of the theoretical model into operative form (school context, materials, teaching procedure, and so on); the continual (formative) *evaluation* of the model in operation; and the *modification* of practice by planned interventions based on the evaluation data gathered. Its basic purpose is to develop the most powerful operative form of the model possible.

Research. Research includes the *identification* or *development* of instruments and methods that can assess the success of the developed program in achieving goals established for it, and can determine its success in comparison with other programs; the implementation of the *terminal assessment* program; and a conclusive, *diagnostic statement* about the program, identifying its strengths, weaknesses, and relative values with a recommendation for implementation, further development, or abandonment. Its basic purpose is to determine the value of the program in competition with other influences on students' learning and development.

Communication and Implementation. This final phase requires the development of *strategies* for introducing recommended programs into particular schools and districts; *pilot studies* to analyze sources of resistance and to develop methods of resolving them; and *implementation.* The basic purpose is to introduce the new program in such a way that the chance of failure for reasons not directly relevant to the nature of the program is minimized. And the process begins again. (This process is described in greater detail in Gibbons, 1970.)

This monograph is a preliminary and tentative attempt to pursue the first of these stages, analyzing the various forms of individualized instruction to establish some consistency of terminology, creating a basis for organizing the programs to reveal the relationships among them, and developing a framework for describing them from a consistent point of view. This analysis is only the first of the five stages in the process described above, and should be considered in that perspective.

TWO

CLASSIFYING THE PROGRAMS

Sources of Confusion

There are many varieties of individualized programs. The groups of individualized programs overlap and mix individualizing features so randomly that the Winnetka Plan, for instance, can be referred to as individualization through grouping, a self-paced program, independent study, individually prescribed instruction, tutorial, and so on. Identifying programs as individualized conveys so little information about them that any teacher can on some grounds claim to be individualizing instruction. Before programs can be described and compared in any systematic way that clearly distinguishes one from another, some of the reasons for this confusion must be recognized and resolved. Many of the ambiguities seem to be inherent in the term itself.

First, *individualized instruction* suggests a contra-distinction to *non-individualized instruction*, but it is im-

15

possible to un-individualize instruction. Every program is unavoidably individualized to some degree by the perception each person has of it and the response he makes to it. Second, when an administrator or teacher increases the number of alternatives open to every student, he may be said to have individualized instruction, but the individualization will be relative and possible rather than absolute or necessary. A program cannot make students more individualistic. It can only increase the opportunities for each of them to express and develop the unique characteristics he brings to bear on any program—the habits, history, perception, sensitivity, curiosity, anxiety, intelligence, and imagination that individualize any instruction. Does not a lecture to a thousand students "provide ideas against which each man can measure his own, and information from which each may draw his own conclusion?" Third, different aspects of individualized instruction are emphasized by different people, depending on their role in the schooling process. Principals may be concerned about the organization of classes, teachers by the availability of materials and the degree of informality required, students by the changes in the level and nature of effort required, and so on. The result is that descriptions are slanted to the different perspectives of different writers so that the same program may sound very different in a selection of reports about it. To describe the program the point of view must be clearly fixed—the administrator's, the teacher's, or the student's—and the description must be in operational terms.

Another source of confusion is the dual meaning of the word "individualized." An individualized program may be thought of as separate instruction for each person, or as instruction that more closely approaches separate teaching for each person than did some previous program. In other words, a tutorial may be described as individualized instruction, and teaching a class of twenty-five when the class size was formerly thirty may also be so described. Referring to students by name when no recognition was previously given may also be referred to as individualization. If any program may be described as individualized, the central question becomes, "To what degree has separate instruction been accomplished?" Any description, to be valuable, should provide a basis for locating each program on a scale, indicating in some way the extent to which individualization, as defined in the proposal, has been achieved.

Designing a scale, however, is complicated by three factors. First, the special treatment may be applied to selected elements rather than exhaustively to all the elements of an instructional program. One approach may permit each student to work at his own pace while all students are required to study the same content with the same materials in the same way in the same place to the same standard and by the same method of teaching. Another program may offer or permit personal alternatives in all of these elements. Second, the elements chosen may be individualized to different degrees. For instance, the teacher may individualize the subject-matter component by allowing members of different groups to read different texts, by allowing each student to select his own books on a subject, by allowing him to choose books on any topic, or by allowing him to pursue any interest through any materials. Third, individualized instruction may refer to a program that is individualized for only a small part of the school day or week, or one that involves only a few carefully selected students. The other part of the program, or the general school program, may be rigidly teacher-directed mass instruction. A report can too easily suggest large-scale reconstruction of schooling when, in fact, the supervisor has merely been removed from the study hall period for selected seniors. A course description, then, should distinguish which elements are being indivualized, to what degree, for what portion of school time, and for what portion of the student body.

How can such a course description be accomplished? In the remainder of this chapter an attempt will be made to lay some groundwork for a solution to the problem. It will involve two stages: (1) an elementary classification of existing programs, and (2) an analysis of the distinguishing elements of an instructional program as the categories of a crude profile for contrasting curriculum proposals.

Elementary Classification of Existing Programs

Individualized instruction represents not a species or genus but a family, an order, even a phylum of curriculum programs. Classifying them into mutually exclusive categories and organizing sub-categories so that the pattern explains relationships among them requires clear-cut boundaries on the field of investigation and a consistent focus for examining the programs. To avoid contending with the whole range of self-instructional experiences and non-deliberative or spontaneous learning experiences (Stephens, 1967) that can arise from any aspect of daily life, the field of investigation should be limited to school learning experiences, and more particularly to learning experiences resulting from some intentional agency on the part of faculty and administration.

From what point of view should programs be examined? Selecting a focus of analysis for description in general and classification in particular is complicated by alternative choices: the philosophy on which the program is based, the administration of the program, the learning strategies employed by the teacher, or the student's perception, i.e., the actual learning that results from the program. If an appropriate point of view is not chosen and sustained, a common occurrence in the curriculum literature, intention is too easily confused with achievement.

The philosophy or theory is a weak focus, since it may shape a program, merely justify it, or be a wishful statement completely unrelated to practice and accomplishment. Seldom, if ever, is the stated philosophy fully realized in the program supposedly derived from it. Such terms as "freedom," "independence," and "self-direction" have so many forms and degrees in practice that interpretation is confounded. Helen Parkhurst (1922), for instance, states on one page that the ideal school is "a community whose essential condition is freedom for the individual to develop himself" (p. 18), and on the next states that, for the student, "Freedom is taking his own time." Yet, the student must take someone else's content, in someone else's order, under someone else's conditions, according to someone else's standards. These impositions are apparently not considered to be violations of his freedom. The advocates who claim that freedom and individualization should be accomplished through groups also demonstrate how far short of achieving stated ideals a practice may fall. Another example is the suggestion for individualization by DeHaan and Doll (1964, p. 21) that a teacher "can find at least a few opportunities to point out the personal relevance of the ongoing activities to the lives of pupils." These authors also illustrate one other shortcoming of a philosophical focus: that enthusiasts may ascribe to such a practice as individualization the

fulfillment of ideals that have at best oblique relationship
to it.

We believe that individualization of teaching is increased when
education relies as much as possible upon reality and upon actual
experience for its content. Observations, firsthand experiences,
and direct contacts with the world are the raw material of education (p. 20).

Tracing historical origins would provide an equally
weak focus for categorization. Different styles of individualization have emerged to reform traditional practices,
but as Lawrence Cremin (1961, p. 8) observes:

. . . reform movements are notoriously ahistorical in outlook.
They look forward rather than back; and when they do need a
history, they frequently prefer the fashioning of ideal ancestors
to the acknowledgement of mortals.

Even this cursory examination tends to support his argument.

Administrative policy does change the learning experience by modifying the relationship among teachers and
between teacher and students, as occurs in the change-
over from class instruction to team teaching. But administration can ultimately only organize the framework in
which classroom instruction and individual learning take
place. Change in students is the fundamental purpose of
individualization, but great individual differences among
them make their responses widely varied, largely un-
known, and, therefore, another distorted focus for cate-
gorizing programs. In fact, it is an irony of the literature
that many who labor to focus instruction on the individual evaluate their success with group tests that measure gains on one dimension, or a narrow spectrum of
dimensions, of accomplishment. The teacher's objectives

are also a weak basis of organization. They are more often fond hopes than operationally defined directives for instruction and evaluation. And even those precisely stated may be achieved by a variety of instructional means. But what the teacher actually does can be stipulated, observed, and reported—what he provides, what he demands or allows, what role he plays, and, generally, in what way he modifies traditional methods or adapts instruction to each child separately. For this reason the nature of the conditions for learning provided by the teacher, from whatever source of inspiration or authority, seems the most reliable basis for describing a program.

From this point of view, what are the fundamental distinctions among the forms of individualization? The two most inclusive subgroups of all programs that claim to be individualized seem to be those in which the teacher regularly directs instruction to each student separately in some way, and those in which the teacher generally addresses the same form of instruction to more than one student, to groups. Usually referred to as *individual* and *individualized,* respectively, the latter form is more accurately and less ambiguously called *class* or *group* instruction, since the term *individualized* is applied to both families of programs, personal and group (see Figure 1). Individualization through group approaches is at best the amelioration of ills inherent in mass instruction. It cannot lead to the abolition of them. Group approaches, at their worst, involve such token changes they become apologies for the inadequacies they profess to resolve. Given that instruction is conducted in groups, some systems are undoubtedly better than others, and, for accomplishing certain kinds of goals, may be superior to all other programs. The central concern here, however, is with instruction addressed to individual students.

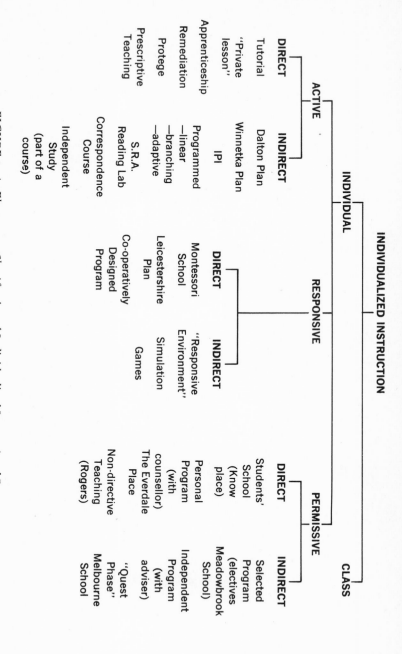

FIGURE 1. An Elementary Classification of Individualized Instructional Programs

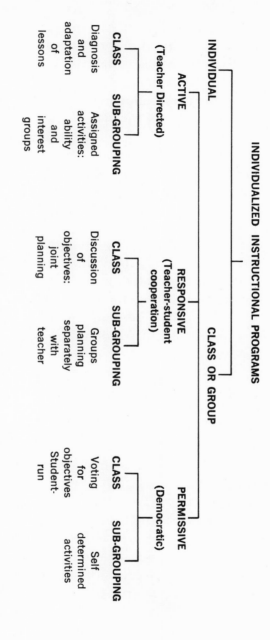

FIGURE 2. A Rough Classification of Individualization through Group Practices

Whereas the first subdivision is based on how the teacher addresses his students, the second subdivision is based upon the decision-making pattern the teacher establishes in the classroom. Is he *actively* in control, making all but a few decisions? Is he *permissive* in the instructional program, allowing or encouraging the student to make the most of his own curriculum decisions? Or does his approach lie between these extremes? Is he *responsive,* planning co-operatively and always on hand to respond to questions and requests? The distinction between active and permissive teacher roles in decision-making is more vividly described by Sidney Jourard, in *The Theory and Nature of Independent Learning* (Gleason, 1967, pp. 82–84), as the roles of "Commissar" and "Guru." One imposes dependence, the other makes independence possible. For the student it means no less than the difference between "learning for others" and "learning for himself." As such it becomes the crucial focus for any discussion of student freedom, responsibility, and initiative developed within the school curriculum. In *active* forms of individualization, instruction may be modified for each student but still include any of the constraints on individual freedom typical of the traditional classroom. The following are examples:

1. Constraint to attend.
2. Constraint to accept given company of adults and peers.
3. Constraint to submit and obey.
4. Constraint to act in routine ways and by schedule.
5. Constraint to address given material, relevant or irrelevant.
6. Constraint to sustain address to a lesson irrespective of interest or judgment.
7. Constraint to treat material in a given way, to select as directed.

8. Constraint to respond and to agree.
9. Constraint to wait.
10. Constraint to learn and present in a given way.
11. Constraint to discontinue learning and to defer learning.
12. Constraint to accept another person's judgment and standard of judgment.
13. Constraint to accept the specific objectives and goals of another.
14. Constraint to study material already mastered.
15. Constraint to keep pace with a class or group.

Teachers working within the framework of permissive individualized programs may remove as many of these constraints as the administrative structure allows. Obviously, more constraints are removed in Summerhill's program than in individually prescribed instruction; more are removed in Leicestershire's approach to schooling than in programmed instruction.

The degree to which students are prepared for, and permitted to participate in, the development of their own curricula also demonstrates the epistemological, psychological, and pedagogical assumptions underlying the teaching method. For instance, *actively* specifying what is to be learned implies the assumption that there is an identifiable body of knowledge, experience, or skills essential to every student, and that it has in fact been identified. Specifying when or in what sequence the chosen subject matter is to be learned implies that a certain logical order of knowledge or skill development replicates the optimal psychological order of learning for each person. Specifying the method by which the child will learn seems to assume that there is a universal style by which the desired behavior can or should be imposed. Permissive teaching implies the assumption that content, sequence of learning, structure of knowledge, and learning style are, or should be, individual and personal, and therefore cannot be presented. When the autonomy of the student emerges as a primary consideration, aspects of the learning process other than content mastery become important:

1. Deciding what is worth learning and what is not.
2. Deciding what degree of difficulty in the task can and cannot be mastered.
3. Deciding how it can best be learned.
4. Generalizing from learning which technique has proved successful.
5. Integrating learning into a personal schema of categories.
6. Determining when learning is complete and when it is incomplete.
7. Recognizing when learning can be applied in areas other than the one in which it is learned.
8. Making imaginative relationships between fields (metaphor, analogy, invention, insight—creative behavior, bisociation).
9. Judging the public and personal worth of what has been learned.
10. Developing ability to generate ideas and activity.
11. Modification of behavior and thinking and study in light of experience.

The measure of quality in *active* decision-making is the efficiency, measured by achievement tests, with which the teacher stimulates students to accomplish objectives he has set for them. *Permissive* teaching, in which students make most of the decisions, runs the risk of being less efficient but broadens the range of experience, permits learning to progress in different ways, with different materials, at different speeds, for different purposes, and with different kinds of results. What is most important, it permits a student to achieve success in a variety of ways without depriving others of their opportunity for recognition. Ironically, the quality of such programs is usually measured by student achievement on traditional tests that have little to do with the purposes given for *permissive* teaching.

The *responsive* teacher in some ways combines these two modes. Although the student may have a choice of materials or a choice of what he does with a given set of materials, the environment and what it contains are usually carefully chosen to stimulate the student in certain ways. Although the teacher does not direct the student, he may question the student during activities or stand by to respond and to encourage the student to go further in exploring the possibilities of his activity. Although the *class* form of individualization is not of central concern here, it should be pointed out that it, too, may be sub-categorized as *active* or teacher-controlled, *responsive* or guided by teacher-student co-operative planning, and *permissive* or democratic, the students determining what the class will learn or do (see Figure 2).

In the first order division of individualization, *individual* and *class* programs were separated. In the second order division *active, responsive,* and *permissive* programs were differentiated within both groups. In the third order of classification one useful basis for separating programs is the basic means by which the teacher instructs: *directly* by confrontation with the student or *indirectly* through such mediating devices as teaching machines, general equipment, study materials, activities, games, simulation, and so on. Although this is a useful basis for separating *individual* programs, it provides for little further differentiation among *class* individualized programs. In such cases a more useful subdivision would separate sub-

grouping practices from main group practices for each of
active, responsive, and *permissive* forms of class teaching. Where the teacher is *actively* directing activities for
all students according to his own plans, for instance,
the subgroups would receive relative individualization
through directed remedial and make-up groups, assigned
project or activity groups, teaching ability groups, and so
on. The main group would be individualized by such
approaches as diagnosing students and adapting class
teaching of the curriculum to their general strengths and
weaknesses, by setting separate assignments, and by including work appropriate for the quick and the slow in
any class exercise or test. Similarly, in the *responsive* and
permissive sub-categories of *class* individualized instruction, subgroups and main groups would be ones taught
by methods consistent with the prevailing form of decision making (see Figure 2). Although distinctions
similar to those in individual programs seem to apply,
group forms are not of central importance in this monograph and will not be pursued further.

The distinctions illustrated by the third level of classification are still crude but demonstrate some fundamental differences among programs, differences that have
been said not to exist, and when acknowledged seldom
lead to differentiation among forms of instruction. *Individual* and *class* forms are clearly separated. It seems
that the most common form of individual program involves *active* though *indirect* teacher control of student
decision-making. Most of the programs in that category
offer the student control only over the pace at which he
works. This is a minimal form of individualization and
its value has been challenged. Fred Wilhelms (1962,
p. 66), for instance, comments that:

. . . In curricular plans based upon individual instruction, the individualization has been largely illusory. A considerable mechanistic quality has limited such schemes, and the fact that the individual students came through the successive turnstiles at their own pace has been made to signify more than it actually means.

These kinds of efforts to fit curriculum to all students have produced disappointingly little genuine accommodation to the more fundamental differences of the individual. . . .

It also seems that when programmed learning is assigned —whether in text form or automated; whether linear, branching, or adaptive—it is clearly related to the Dalton, Winnetka, and other contract plans, which permit individualization of the student's learning pace only. In programmed learning the "unit of learning" is much smaller, the "units" more carefully organized in sequence, and the rewards and tests more regular. Independent study belongs in this category when it involves only the completion of specified homework assignments or "packages" of lessons deriving from a particular course.

When independent study involves co-operative planning between teacher and student of what the student will do on his own, or when the student determines his own program and then merely seeks authorization, independent study becomes different in kind. Montessori schools and the general Leicestershire plan stand out from others, emphasizing as they do the use of carefully prepared materials and the oblique, supplementary relationship of the teacher to the actual learning experience. Computerized multi-media environments that offer learning alternatives to students, or to the teacher working with students, are a different breed of "programmed instruction"; and when programs and auto-instructional machines of all kinds are merely made available to the student for self-initiated learning and activity, they become subordinate elements in *permissive* programs. In this last category *direct* interaction between student and teacher is usually at the student's request, and focuses on matters relevant to the development of the student's personality and growth rather than curriculum mastery. The *indirect* permissive programs enable students to develop their own curriculum either by selecting from many available courses or by developing their own courses from available resource materials, people, and equipment.

At the fourth level of classification and beyond, programs should be more precisely categorized as species. Differences among the items under each sub-title (see Figures 1 and 2) suggest further ramification. But most of the distinctions are obvious or have already been noted, and further effort would be made trivial by the creation of many empty sub-classes. Also, although this analysis has clarified some fundamental distinctions, the descriptive and explanatory power of such classifications of curriculum programs remains weak. There is no pattern of recapitulation among them, no organic base for deriving truly inclusive, consistent categories. A program described in theory is usually different, often quite different, in practice. Certainly, teachers or planners most often adapt rather than adopt ideas presented to them. Ultimately, classification, even generalization, is confounded by a prevailing eclecticism in instruction and curriculum, that is, by the absorption of new ideas into a traditional body of educational practices, a process in which the new is transformed into a paler, more widely acceptable teaching procedure.

THREE

DESCRIBING THE PROGRAMS

Elements of Instructional Programs

Programs could be classified at the fourth level of distinction according to the curriculum elements that are individualized in them. But the elements fundamental to individualization vary in the degree to which they have been individualized as well as in kind. A more comprehensive summary, one that will account for these differences in a program, can be achieved by graphically recording the level of individualization in each element. Such a profile (see Profile 1) offers sound advantages: it requires the examination and explanation of each aspect of a program, it distinguishes the unique features of a program, and it facilitates comparisons of different programs. In this preliminary attempt at a graphic presentation, fifteen elements have been isolated by consulting such curriculum specialists as Tyler (1950) and Taba (1962), and by noting the focus of scorn in the works of such school critics as Holt (1967) and Goodman (1966). With the characteristics of a traditional program establishing a baseline, the gradient of individualization increases as the focus narrows to each separate student, and increases still further as the student gains more control over the nature of his program. But increases in individualization do not necessarily lead to increases in value. The point has been made earlier that each increase in the specification of curriculum requires accompanying constraints upon the student's behavior, narrows the range of learning, and diminishes the student's involvement in curriculum decisions. The argument here is not that student independence is desirable or undesirable but rather that student-determined programs are demonstrably more individualized. If a writer claims it is desirable to individualize but presents a program that shows on a profile only token modifications of the traditional, then he should be expected to explain why he does not recommend individualization of all elements to the greatest degree. The assumption that individualization means complete individualization, unless qualified, underlies this attempt to develop a rough descriptive system.

The fifteen elements of instructional programs that have been isolated are:

1. Percentage of the student body.
2. Percentage of the school day.
3. Attendance.
4. Materials for study.
5. Method by which the materials are to be studied.
6. Pace at which the materials are to be studied.
7. Activity that accompanies or follows study.
8. Decision making.
9. Teaching focus.

10. Teaching function.
11. Teaching method.
12. Environment.
13. Time structure.
14. Evaluation.
15. Objectives or purposes.

A brief discussion of these elements follows.

When individualization is available only to a certain portion of the student population for a certain portion of the day, then the effective power of the innovation will be limited proportionately. Such limitations, presuming that individualization is presented as desirable, should be explained, and more important, the program for other students and for the rest of the school day should be described. Gross incompatibility between the two could easily neutralize any possible advantages of individualizing.

Students are usually required by law to attend school until the age of sixteen. In the traditional school they are required by the administration to be in specific supervised classrooms for most of the school day, and they are required by the teacher to remain at specific desks for most of the school period. Since this constraint dominates other elements of instruction, it should be modified in any program espousing student freedom. At Summerhill and The Everdale Place students attend in the sense that they board at the school, but there is no constraint to attend the formal classes offered (Neill, 1960, pp. 4–5; "The Everdale Place: A School Community," p. 87). In many Leicestershire schools, students are required to attend but move freely from room to room (Featherstone, 1967a, p. 15). F. R. Henderson (1964) describes a New Zealand classroom in which students are required to be present but are free to pursue their own activities or join

an activity led by the teacher, if they wish—as they are in
the Montessori and Leicestershire schools—whereas in
traditional schools students spend most of the day syn-
chronized in their studies and closely supervised.

Four closely related elements—the materials for study,
the method by which the materials are to be studied, the
pace at which the materials are to be studied, and the
activity that accompanies or follows study—have been
assigned the same terms of measure. Each activity may be
prescribed for a grade or class as an assigned curriculum
with required readings to be studied in a manner dictated
by questions asked in class or in the textbook and at a
pace set by the slower members of the group. The activity is a common assignment whether exercises, reading,
composition, or a project. At the other three levels, the
substance of each of these elements may be differentiated
for sub-groups and for individuals or it may be determined by the student for himself. In fact, he may make
decisions in two ways, by choosing among alternatives
offered, or by formulating choices for himself. To include
this distinction on the profile, the "individual choice"
square has been sub-divided, the lower half indicating
student selection from offerings, the upper half student
formulation of his own learning activities.

How are decisions actually made in the classroom? Are
they received ready-made from an outside authority or
does the teacher make them? Do teacher and student plan
co-operatively, or does the student have the final word
about what he will do? These three categories reflect the
active, responsive, and *permissive* distinctions made
above.

Focus refers to the broad class of instructional objectives or purposes that seem to be given highest priority
in a particular program. The scale employed is not in-

compatible with the order described in taxonomies of educational objectives (e.g., Bloom, *et al.,* 1956; and Krathwohl, *et al.,* 1964). Although the progression of stages of individualization in this category is open to serious question, if each subsequent stage is thought of as including the previous ones, the upward direction on the profile indicates that the individual student is being empowered with an increasing range of accomplishments required for self-directed learning. The *function* of the teacher refers to the way the teacher handles the student's confrontation with what is to be learned: he may direct the class through every stage of a lesson, controlling what is to be examined and what it means; he may present students with a learning situation and help them to determine what it means to them; or he may guide them in developing and interpreting their own learning situations or merely be available until his assistance is required and sought. Basically, he may act as interpreter of what is to be learned or he may support the student's own search and interpretation. *Method* refers to the means used by the teacher to bring about the desired learning, the accomplishment of educational objectives—whether by drill or explanation, by shaping the lesson so that students may "discover" the intended concept, or by permitting them to shape their own problems and solve them.

Although they are of great importance in individualized programs, the sources available to the teacher or student are impossible to estimate from most reports and would be difficult to record on a profile. But the range of the available environment that is utilized in an instructional program can be estimated, and that range is one indication of the number of alternative settings, the number of resource people, and the freedom of movement possible. The range extends from a desk in the classroom to various locales for study, work, and experience in the community, as suggested by Goodman (1966), Grannis (1964), and Newmann and Oliver (1967). But "community" can now be thought of as more than social interdependence and mutual concern within a narrow geographic local. Just as the media revolution has made instantaneous indirect participation in the global village possible, the revolution in transportation has made rapid direct participation possible also. Education has yet to exploit the possibilities of activity and experience in the community as locale or as world.

The rigid organization of school time into periods places many constraints on teachers and, through them, on students. In the Dalton and Winnetka Plans the day is divided in half, one part highly organized, the other relatively structureless. The fluid pattern, as, for instance, the one used in Leicestershire schools, is a loose organization of changing activities, which students follow if they choose to but at their own time, unprompted by bells. In the extreme all structure is removed in favor of the individual, informally planned day (Yeomans, 1967, p. 12).

Traditionally, grade-wide examinations and classroom tests on the content and skills taught yield marks that rank students and evaluate their achievement. A broader assessment, including all aspects of the student's learning, accounts for greater individual differences in accomplishment, non-verbal as well as verbal. In some programmed courses the number of units completed is reported without value judgment. Other courses involve students in evaluation. Carl Rogers, for instance, argues that the student's estimate of his own achievement is a fundamental part of the learning process (1961, p. 290). Examinations, when they demand common experience among students, serve the system and are the most formidable front-line defense against individualized instruction. Actual independent study could not survive in such a cross-class or cross-grade examination environment.

Attitudes toward education are sometimes polarized into camps with such labels as traditional and progressive, subject-centered and child-centered, education *for* life and education *as* life, the Platonic view and the Aristotelian view (Parker, 1963, p. 62; Thelen, 1963, pp. 34–35). This dichotomy is reflected in the differences between the first two and the last two cells of category fifteen of the basic profile (see Profile 1). Efficient mastery of set content seems to be the central purpose in the most conservative traditional models. Teaching students to understand content, formulate concepts, master skills, and discover principles inductively are more liberal objectives of subject-centered education, reflecting a concern that individuals comprehend as well as master content. The next stage represents a change in emphasis from intellectual to social development. The focus is on the individual but, ironically, to encourage his acceptance of assigned schooling and his adaptation to it. In the final stage the purpose is continuous intellectual and emotional development toward maturity, that is, nurturing the individual's progress through Piaget's stages of cognition and Erikson's stages of the psycho-social cycle, as well as the stages of natural physical growth. It is an inclusive program concerned with the general development of the child as a person.

The profiles discussed in the remainder of this chapter are on pages 61–70 below.

Profiles and Analyses of Instructional Programs

A profile of a program is made by connecting the appropriate cells in each of the columns representing these fifteen elements. The solid line indicates the "shape" of the instructional program. Where only a portion of school time is devoted to the innovations, the other part of the program is represented by a broken profile line. If no information is given about this part, a null hypothesis is invoked: the unexplained portion is assumed to be traditional. It must be emphasized that the profile is a rough instrument providing a summary of information rather than an accurate measurement of each dimension in an instructional program. Since these profiles are based on general descriptions of programs in reports and articles, which often differ in emphasis and detail, and since the incompleteness of description often necessitates inference and interpretation on the part of the profile-maker, some readers will disagree with the level of placement in certain categories on particular profiles. But the disagreements will be localized and discussion of them should be productive in creating a fuller, more accurate "picture" of the program for comparison with other programs that espouse the same educational principles. One other qualification: discussions of curriculum are often anecdotal. In the most rigid program isolated instances of the most liberal and individual approaches are possible. The concern here is with the prevailing emphasis in each category. Finally, education has a long history of confusing objectives pursued with objectives achieved. The profiles are summaries of statements and claims, not performance and accomplishment, which vary with the school, teacher, and class.

The profile does have other uses. It is a handy (rather than powerful) observational instrument for outlining the major features of an individualized program under study in the field. Profiles of theoretical plans can be compared with profiles of the plans in operation. Similarly, someone supervising teachers can use profiles of intended performance and actual performance as a basis for discussion during preparatory and in-service training. A teacher or group of teachers can use profiles to characterize present practice and to outline a plan for individualized instruction. The discussion that follows is concerned with nine profiles derived from written reports and one (Profile 10) that illustrates a secondary use of the profile: the contrast of theory and practice.

The Extremes of Conservatism and Liberalism

The instructional programs in the secondary schools of Watertown, Massachusetts, examined in a Harvard Study (Watertown and the Education of Its Children, 1967), at that time exhibited all the characteristics of the traditional model, the baseline of practice that individualized programs seem to be a reaction against (see Profile 1). The student-run school in Vancouver, British Columbia, called Knowplace (Johnson, 1967, p. 5), exemplifies the most liberal form of individualization. A school established by students when they could win no flexibility from the regular school system, it represents an extreme remodelling of the school concept that is probably not possible within the constraints of institutionalism (see Profile 2). Whereas Watertown High School was, at the time of the study, carefully age-graded and subdivided into homogenous groups on seven different tracks, Knowplace is one "family" group of heterogeneous 12- to 18-

year-olds. Materials, pace, manner of study, and activities were often set for the track, sometimes for the grade, at Watertown, whereas each student at Knowplace determines what he will do when and how and with what and whom he chooses: he may elect to take a regular course (which he completes at any time) or to leave the school for several days to do his own work. Whereas lessons at Watertown were in no way differentiated for individuals, at Knowplace the individual's program may be his own in every possible way. As one of the advisers explains, "Education here is a two-way affair with both students and staff learning from each other in a completely free setting" (Johnson, 1967, p. 5). Other individualized programs fall within the range bounded by these two extremes. If such schools as Watertown's constitute the commonplace lock-step system, against which innovators react, such schools as Knowplace establish an upper limit of freedom and self-direction in education, against which any individualized program founded on these principles must measure its proposals. Two facts, however, must be kept clearly in mind. First, the school was created by certain students who would no longer tolerate the boredom and conformity imposed by a traditional school. The replicability of such a program, the possibility of institutionalizing it, is problematical. Second, this is a descriptive upper limit and not an evaluative one. The conceptualization of schooling seen in Knowplace may be an extreme *form* of individualization, but this does not mean the execution or the results of the program are necessarily exemplary.

Programs Emphasizing Individual Pacing

Profiles 3, 4, 5, and 6 underscore the central importance of individual pacing in Programmed Instruction, Individually Prescribed Instruction (IPI), the Winnetka Plan, and, to a lesser degree, the Dalton Laboratory Plan. Programmed Instruction, as a task assigned to students, seems to individualize pace alone. Adaptive forms make it possible to change program sequences, and to prescribe materials of instruction individually if the system includes several media. But the price of subject-specific objectives, intensive control of the stages of learning, and pursuit of mastery and achievement is the neglect of other dimensions of individualization. There is also the possibility that rote learning common in such programs may only be appropriate when the individual has determined for himself that the content is in some way desirable. Washburne's controlled study at Winnetka (Washburne and Marland, 1963, pp. 58–63), for instance, demonstrates that formal learning begun too early may be detrimental to later progress. In IPI the unit rather than the frame is the basic element of instruction, but the pattern remains essentially the same.

In the Oakleaf Project, a major study of IPI originating at the University of Pittsburgh, the major modification appears to be, as the profile illustrates, the freedom of each student to move through assigned units of curriculum at his own rate. At the beginning of the year he is thoroughly tested for placement in the sequence of self-study materials (mostly mimeographed sheets) he must complete. During the year only the morning is devoted to IPI in reading, science, and mathematics, whereas the afternoon is spent in the regular district program. The student-teacher relationship is described this way:

This type of individual study is done at a desk in a study area seating 80 or 90 pupils. In this room, besides the other pupils, there will be two or three teachers to provide instructional assistance and three or four clerks to distribute materials and grade papers. Most pupils are able to proceed through their study materials with only a minimum of help from the teachers. If a teacher finds a pupil who needs more help than she can give in this large group situation, this pupil is directed to a small side room where another teacher will give him more extensive individual help or will involve him in small group instruction (The Project for Individually Prescribed Instruction, p. 8).

The basic assumptions on which the program has been developed underline the emphasis on behavioral objectives, pace, and testing:

1. One obvious way in which pupils differ is in the amount of time and practice that it takes to master given instructional objectives.

2. One important aspect of providing for individual differences is to arrange conditions so that each student can work through the sequence of instructional units at his own pace and with the amount of practice that he needs.

3. If a school has the proper types of study materials, elementary school pupils, working in a tutorial environment which emphasizes self-learning, can learn with a minimum amount of direct teacher instruction.

4. In working through a sequence of instructional units, no pupil should be permitted to start work on a new unit until he has acquired a specified minimum degree of mastery of the material in the units identified as prerequisite to it.

5. If pupils are to be permitted and encouraged to proceed at individual rates, it is important for both the individual pupil and for the teacher that the program provide for frequent evaluations of pupil progress which can provide a basis for the development of individual instructional prescriptions (The Project for Individually Prescribed Instruction, pp. 3–4).

In this program the only element individualized is pace, which is maximized for each student so that he can fulfill set objectives and complete materials efficiently (see Profile 3). The so-called tutorial element is indistinguishable from teacher-assistance in any classroom where students are doing a common exercise. The idea that converting the teacher's spoken word to type and lesson sequences to packaged materials constitutes a breakthrough to "self-learning" is not credible. Further, the program falls far short of the possibilities of prescribing programs particularly appropriate for the individual that the title of the system implies. Diagnosis is employed but only to place the student appropriately in the series of lessons in each subject (and as such is another dimension of pacing), and not as a basis for determining appropriate objectives, materials, activities, procedures, or modifications of any of the other instructional elements for each individual. Since this half of instruction is apparently very academic, the nature of the afternoon program is doubly important, but it is described only as the regular program for the district, a condition that invokes the null hypothesis.

Carleton Washburne describes his modification of Frederic Burk's theories in these words:

If any part of the education of Winnetka can legitimately be called "The Winnetka Plan" it is this principle of distinction between (a) individual mastery of skills and (b) group and creative activities, and the techniques for developing both *and* assuring their interaction (Washburne and Marland, 1963, p. 107).

The "tool subjects" (arithmetic, reading, and the language arts) were taught by dividing the curriculum into units of achievement that all students were required to master (the solid line in Profile 5). Diagnostic testing was used to identify which students should begin a new unit or receive special assistance. The units assigned were basically "self-instructive self-corrective practice materials" that the student completed at his own pace. As in IPI, the teacher was on hand to provide added assistance. This system was carried over in part to social studies and science, but these subjects seemed to be best acquired "incidentally in a rich program of activities, visual aids, reading and discussion" (Washburne and Marland, p. 81). The other half of the Winnetka Plan, the group and creative activities, included projects, drama, music, clubs, electives, physical education and recreation, the practice of citizenship and democracy, and school assemblies (the broken line in Profile 5). In these activities, each child had room to exercise his special interests and talents, but each was to coordinate his special interests with those of others toward a common end. Whereas materials for "the common essentials" were prepared with an extraordinary amount of care and effort, the academic program was similar to other subject-matter-centered, self-paced programs and to the "student packets" being developed for some independent study proposals. The group and creative activities seem typical of other efforts to "individualize" through group projects. The assumption that the two kinds of schooling would interact and become integrated in the student's life is a speculation common to all theories involving the analysis of desirable behavior into its constituents for separate training.

Study under the Dalton Laboratory Plan (see Profile 6) required signing a jobbing "contract" for work in each subject. The student received an outline of the total requirement for the subject and short-term units that explained the task, provided references, and stated a particular exercise or activity to be completed. Subject matter was not the specific statement of a program frame or precise test-like materials more common in IPI and Winnetka units, but rather whatever resources would help the student resolve the problem set. Some problems were exact ("What was Piraeus?"), some involved activities ("Draw a plan of the front of the Parthenon"),

others were general and imaginative ("You are a reporter
. . . assigned to write up the Battle of Bosworth Field").
Precise records were kept by faculty and by students of
units completed, but students were free to spend as much
time or as little as they wished in the laboratories set up
for each subject. In the laboratory all materials appropriate for the subject were collected and study was
guided by a specialist. How, where, and when the work
was done was not dictated as long as contracts were met.
Although there was variety within the units, all subjects
were taught in this way, including art and music. Weekly
recitations and group meetings guaranteed regular con-
tact with each child, and students needing extra help or
groups at the same stage were called out often for tutorials
or group discussions. It is clear from the profile that
students were given more freedom and responsibility than
in the previous three programs. Under Helen Parkhurst,
even the pressure of examinations was relaxed in favor of
a report on the work completed (Parkhurst, 1922, p.
140). But the faculty made all the major curriculum
decisions. There was no suggestion that the student was
free not to contract any course or unit prescribed for him.
It seems that the student was more or less forced to make
the commitment, which was then used more or less to
force him to do the work. As in the other three programs,
mastery of specific content and skills is the fundamental
educative task; pace is the most common variable—per-
haps because it increases the apparent efficiency of the
class. Constant testing, checking, and recording are examples of the constraints still deemed necessary to insure
accomplishment.

Time and Resources: Independent Study Programs

In "Independent Study—for *all* Students" (Glatthorn and Ferderbar, 1966) the authors describe a program involving 97 percent of the student body at Abington High School for 25 percent of their school time (see Profile 7). In his independent study time "the student has almost complete freedom of choice as to where he studies, what he works on, and what kind of assistance he secures" (p. 379). A wide range of resources are available in appropriate laboratory or study commons supervised by specialists or para-professionals. Students may choose to spend some of their independent time in large group lectures, which are part of regular courses, or in short-run electives. Intensive remedial clinics (over 100 per week), special programs in basic skills, and conferences are given but attendance seems to be mandatory rather than optional. What the authors mean by freedom of choice in what the student works on seems to confuse two very distinct levels of freedom: freedom to choose from among tasks that must be done, and freedom to determine one's own task. If, as they report, only "about 10% of . . . students . . . are ready to take on original research projects" (p. 380), then the rest of independent study must be largely extra practice or in-school "homework." Indeed, such independent learning activities as these are offered as typical: "getting remedial help," "typing a report," "doing advanced work on a project," and "working on a programmed text." If students are only selecting the *order* in which they complete assignments they are constrained to complete under the threat of losing school privileges, independence is severely limited and misrepresented. This ambiguity is emphasized by the profile. It *appears* that the independent portion of the program is quite individualized, whereas, in fact, it may *not* be (broken line). Also, the regular program may be very formal, and may dominate "independent" activities. These circumstances again underscore the need for a precise vocabulary and a frame of reference for developing individualized programs.

In fairness, it should be pointed out that this analysis is based on one article, not on observation, and that changes have occurred at Abington since the article was written.

Leicestershire Schools

Profile 8 suggests that education in Leicestershire is highly individualized for every student, whether he adjusts immediately to the freedom permitted him or not. During the free or integrated day there is "no real difference between one subject in the curriculum and another, or even between work and play" (Featherstone, 1967a). In a few schools students may be in "family" groups of children of various ages, and in all schools they will each have a wide choice of materials and activities—some commercially produced, many home-made—to which they can devote their attention when and for as long as they wish, limited only by the demand for the materials by other students. Although some teachers may insist on some regular reading and writing, there are generally no required subjects and no required assignments upon which students must, at some time, concentrate.[1] Students learn from their activities, from other children, and from the guidance of the teachers. They move freely from one

[1] I am indebted to Charles Rathbone for a first-hand report of his observation in several Leicestershire schools. He found great variety in the degree to which teachers actually practiced the idealized Leicestershire program.

area in the school to another. The degree of independence evident in this program contrasts markedly with that of so-called "independent" study, even though activities are selected rather than student-initiated, and therefore involve less than maximum individual control. Nor is independence offered in combination with traditional courses; the program is consistent and sustained. Many other constraints are also minimized. There are no examinations or report cards as such. Rather parents receive detailed "histories" reporting what the student has accomplished (p. 20). Discipline is relaxed and when a student causes a disturbance the teacher attempts to find more appropriate materials and approaches rather than deny the privilege of independence to the student who may need it most. This form of individualization is not isolated to a few schools. The recent Plowden Committee's Report, *Children and their Primary Schools* (1967), indicates that fully one-third of British primary and some secondary schools have been influenced by the new ideas (p. 20).

Summerhill

Schools in the Summerhill mold have a split program, just as schools operating on the Winnetka model and those offering IPI or independent study have (see Profile 9). But there are, nevertheless, marked differences. Regular morning instruction is traditional in character at Summerhill, with two important exceptions: attendance is entirely optional, and students in the weekly "town meeting" can speak and vote for changes in most aspects of school life, including curriculum and teaching. Summerhill is a self-governing school in all but matters of health and safety. The activities of the afternoon are decided individually and are pursued without supervision unless desired, wherever the student chooses to play or work—in school, on the grounds, or in the community. The central theme is freedom, without apologetic claims of increased responsibility, a marked contrast to the prescriptive practices already described:

The function of the child is to live his own life—not the life his anxious parents think he should live, nor a life according to the purpose of the educator who thinks he knows what is best. All this interference and guidance on the part of adults only produces a generation of robots (Neill, 1960, p. 12).

Although the instructional program is directive, then, the student always has control over his own behavior, even though he may be punished by his peers for breaking their rules or summoned to a "private lesson," a chat with the Headmaster, if troubles accumulate. The unique influence of such a teacher as Neill may be the most important element in the success of a program, but it cannot be captured on a profile. Whatever that influence is, it has nothing to do with methodological innovations:

We have no new methods of teaching, because we do not consider that teaching matters very much. Whether a school has or has not a special method for teaching long division is of no significance, for long division is of no importance except to those who *want* to learn it. And the child who *wants* to learn long division *will* learn it no matter how it is taught (Neill, 1960, p. 5).

For this reason Neill may have a great deal to teach educators about parenthood and about relating to children, but he does not offer a model for instruction. Despite what he suggests, oppressive traditionalism is not the only alternative to the free, progressive school.

Profiles of Practice

Inevitably the theorist's communication of a model to others will be incomplete. The model, based on many substrata of experience, cannot be conveyed in the fullness of conviction and principle. The debates that preceded its formulation cannot be represented. All the details for application cannot be supplied. The administrator or teacher, even given a complete description, will be required to interpret its meaning, to translate its principles into classroom action. During any of these stages of transfer from theory to practice there will be a strong tendency to regress toward the familiar. In the end it will be quite possible that the theory presented by the teacher will change but instruction itself will remain virtually as it was. Once a profile of an instructional program has been agreed upon it can serve the implementation of the program in two ways. It can be used to communicate the nature of the program to teachers (in articles or discussion) and, if a profile of the teacher's actual practice is drawn based on observation, the general ways in which the teacher (or school faculty) is misinterpreting the model can be isolated and discussed.[2] Profile 10 illustrates the difference between the theoretical profile of the Leicestershire program (the solid line) and the practice by a teacher who was attempting to implement that theory (the broken line).

The profile may also be useful in teacher supervision, particularly of practice teachers. This would not solve the problem of determining ideal instructional methods, but would facilitate summarization of the student teach-

[2] I am indebted to Prof. Courtney Cazden of Harvard University for the idea that the profile could be used as a gross observational tool.

er's instructional behavior as "feedback," and would isolate dimensions for discussion. The profile is not intended to be sacrosanct and could be made more detailed by adding categories or subdividing existing ones, or less detailed by grouping or eliminating categories to suit the user's purpose. A detailed description may be more useful in teacher development than a graded evaluation that is based on the indescribable and indefensible subjective criteria of "experience" so widely practiced as supervision.

FOUR

CONCLUSION

This volume began with the proposition that the term *individualized instruction* is used, or may be used, to refer to such a variety of instructional programs that it has little meaning. To differentiate among the programs and to clarify underlying differences, an elementary classification and a profiling system were introduced. Profiles of a few individualized instructional programs were compared and found to be widely different in the kind and degree of individualization they involved.

In the course of developing a system for describing the unique features of curriculum proposals, a number of complicating factors were identified:

1. The term *individualized instruction* is used to describe both minute changes in conventional teaching and changes involving the complete reconstruction of schooling.
2. The term is inherently ambiguous, suggesting anything from separate education for each stu-

53

dent to any degree of modification of mass instruction.

3. Every program is individualized by the perception and response of the individual; or, no program can do more than shape the conditions for learning.

4. Describing the nature of individualization from different points of view (theorist, historian, administrator, teacher, student) leads to different conclusions.

5. Individualized programs vary in the elements of instruction they individualize and the degree of individualization in those elements.

6. The theoretical or philosophical reasons offered for change are seldom fully realized in the proposal that results; rather they are explained or justified as improvements of traditional practice.

7. The individualized instructional program may be offered to only a portion of the student body for a portion of the school time.

In addition, several fundamental differences among groups of programs were isolated:

1. Some programs offer ways of instructing students separately, others provide ways of differentiating among students during group or class instruction.

2. Some programs individualize by more precise control of the student through instruction, others by transferring to the student more control over instruction.

3. In some programs the teacher is directive (active), in others he is responsive, and in others he is relatively passive (permissive).

4. In some programs instruction depends directly on teacher-student interaction, in others the teacher is involved indirectly through the materials or environment he has created for the student.

To identify more specific differences among individualized programs, it was suggested:

1. That significant elements of instructional programs be isolated and described for each program.
2. That the description be concerned only with the
   learning situation actually created for the student
   by the teacher.
3. That the description focus on the degree to which
   each element had been individualized.
4. That the degree grows greater as attention is nar-
   rowed from class to group to individual, and that
   it grows greater still as prescriptions for the individual student give way to choices and, finally,
   to the allocation of full responsibility to the student.
5. That when programs are only reported in part,
   the null instructional hypothesis should be invoked: that the neglected portion should be considered lock-step mass instruction.

Several conclusions are suggested by these attempts to
describe individualized instructional programs:

1. A precise vocabulary is needed to establish accurate communication about instruction. Such a
   classification as the one begun here may form a
   basis for a useful taxonomy.
2. Programs should be conceived, practiced, and reported in all their dimensions, and with a full
   qualification of the degree to which the authors
   attempt to achieve the purposes they present.
3. A program of instruction should be coherent
   horizontally, in all its elements, and vertically, for
   students of all ages.

Recent studies have seriously challenged the importance of curriculum changes. In *Equality of Educational
Opportunity,* for instance, James Coleman concludes:

It appears that variations in the facilities and curriculums of the schools account for relatively little variation in pupil achievement insofar as this is measured by standard tests (1966, p. 21).

And J. M. Stephens, after reviewing the relevant research, finds that variations in curriculum plans, teaching methods, size and organization of classes, school facilities—in fact, schooling in general—make little difference in children's over-all achievement (1967). He attributes this general uniformity of results from different methods of education to spontaneous factors of learning common to every child's experience at home and in school, factors so fundamental that relatively superficial, institutional changes do not significantly alter their effects. No one involved in curriculum development can afford to ignore the implications of these conclusions: first, that the constraints on individuals to learn prescribed content in specific ways should not be considered necessary conditions for achievement. Second, that if major curriculum changes make little difference in accomplishment, tinkering with a few hours of independent study, or the like, certainly cannot be counted on to make students self-determining learners. Third, if achievement is stable through curriculum change, this may be interpreted as a sanction to create a program that gives priority to criteria other than marketable accomplishments.

What then is individualized instruction? Not one program, or kind of program, but many programs and kinds of programs. It is a movement, a liberal movement. The spectrum of programs embraced by the movement begins on the right with the amelioration of mass teaching, and shifts to the left by concentration on group practices, adaptation of subject matter to the individual, and, finally, by emancipation of the student from the constraints of education planned by others. Most proposals suggest that education for separate individuals is desirable. Whereas one group of theorists continues the search for the perfect input to yield predicted outputs, a larger group argues that independence, self-direction, initiative, freedom, and responsibility must be developed in students. In a moratorium that permits subordination of the standardized-achievement motive and suspension of teachers' anxiety about control, the opportunity arises to develop a coherent instructional program that tolerates and nurtures widely divergent goals and accomplishments, a program designed to prepare students for complete control of their own education so that schooling, ultimately, is inseparable from living. This, a study of the programs suggests, is the utopia of individualized instruction. A model for creating, developing, and evaluating such a utopia has yet to be designed.

PROFILES

1.	PERCENTAGE OF STUDENT BODY				
2.	PERCENTAGE OF SCHOOL TIME				
3.	ATTENDANCE	Optional	School Not Class	Class Not Sub-Group	Mandatory
4.	MATERIALS FOR STUDY	Individual Choice	Individual Prescribed		
5.	METHOD OF STUDYING MATERIALS	Individual Choice	Individual Prescribed		
6.	PACE OF STUDY	Individual Choice	Individual Prescribed	Sub-Group Prescribed Or Discussed	Class/Grade Prescribed
7.	ACTIVITY	Individual Choice	Individual Prescribed	Sub-Group Prescribed Or Discussed	Class/Grade Prescribed
8.	DECISION-MAKING	Student (Permissive)	Student and Teacher (Responsive)	Teacher (Active)	Administrative Authority
9.	TEACHING FOCUS	Values	Processes	Skill Concepts	Content
10.	TEACHING FUNCTION	Teacher Available	Teacher Guides	Teacher Presents	Teacher Directs
11.	TEACHING METHOD	Unspecified Discovery (Permissive)	Guided Discovery (Problem Solving)	Explanation and Discussion	Drill Exercise Repetition
12.	ENVIRONMENT	Community	School	Classroom or Resource Area	Desk
13.	TIME STRUCTURE	Non-Structured	Fluid	Structured Non-Structured	Structured
14.	EVALUATION	Student Self-Evaluation	Broad Assessment	Quantity Of Work	Exam-Class Rank
15.	PURPOSES OF PROGRAM	Continuous Development To Maturity	Adjustment	Understanding	Efficient Mastery

Profile 1: Watertown High School (1966-1967): A Traditional Humanities Program

1.	PERCENTAGE OF STUDENT BODY				
2.	PERCENTAGE OF SCHOOL TIME				
3.	ATTENDANCE	Optional	School Not Class	Class Not Sub-Group	Mandatory
4.	MATERIALS FOR STUDY	Individual Choice	Individual Prescribed	Sub-Group Prescribed Or Discussed	Class/Grade Prescribed
5.	METHOD OF STUDYING MATERIALS	Individual Choice	Individual Prescribed	Sub-Group Prescribed Or Discussed	Class/Grade Prescribed
6.	PACE OF STUDY	Individual Choice	Individual Prescribed	Sub-Group Prescribed Or Discussed	Class/Grade Prescribed
7.	ACTIVITY	Individual Choice	Individual Prescribed	Sub-Group Prescribed Or Discussed	Class/Grade Prescribed
8.	DECISION-MAKING	Student (Permissive)	Student and Teacher (Responsive)	Teacher (Active)	Administrative Authority
9.	TEACHING FOCUS	Values	Processes	Skill Concepts	Content
10.	TEACHING FUNCTION	Teacher Available	Teacher Guides	Teacher Presents	Teacher Directs
11.	TEACHING METHOD	Unspecified Discovery (Permissive)	Guided Discovery (Problem Solving)	Explanation and Discussion	Drill Exercise Repetition
12.	ENVIRONMENT	Community	School	Classroom or Resource Area	Desk
13.	TIME STRUCTURE	Non-Structured	Fluid	Structured Non-Structured	Structured
14.	EVALUATION	Student Self-Evaluation	Broad Assessment	Quantity Of Work	Exam-Class Rank
15.	PURPOSES OF PROGRAM	Continuous Development To Maturity	Adjustment	Understanding	Efficient Mastery

Profile 2. Knowplace: A Student-Run School 1967-68

1.	PERCENTAGE OF STUDENT BODY				
2.	PERCENTAGE OF SCHOOL TIME				
3.	ATTENDANCE	Optional	School Not Class	Class Not Sub-Group	Mandatory
4.	MATERIALS FOR STUDY	Individual Choice	Individual Prescribed	Sub-Group Prescribed Or Discussed	Class/Grade Prescribed
5.	METHOD OF STUDYING MATERIALS	Individual Choice	Individual Prescribed	Sub-Group Prescribed Or Discussed	Class/Grade Prescribed
6.	PACE OF STUDY	Individual Choice	Individual Prescribed	Sub-Group Prescribed Or Discussed	Class/Grade Prescribed
7.	ACTIVITY	Individual Choice	Individual Prescribed	Sub-Group Prescribed Or Discussed	Class/Grade Prescribed
8.	DECISION-MAKING	Student (Permissive)	Student and Teacher (Responsive)	Teacher (Active)	Administrative Authority
9.	TEACHING FOCUS	Values	Processes	Skill Concepts	Content
10.	TEACHING FUNCTION	Teacher Available	Teacher Guides	Teacher Presents	Teacher Directs
11.	TEACHING METHOD	Unspecified Discovery (Permissive)	Guided Discovery (Problem Solving)	Explanation and Discussion	Drill Exercise Repetition
12.	ENVIRONMENT	Community	School	Classroom or Resource Area	Desk
13.	TIME STRUCTURE	Non-Structured	Fluid	Structured Non-Structured	Structured
14.	EVALUATION	Student Self-Evaluation	Broad Assessment	Quantity Of Work	Exam-Class Rank
15.	PURPOSES OF PROGRAM	Continuous Development To Maturity	Adjustment	Understanding	Efficient Mastery

Not Clarified

Profile 3: Individually Prescribed Instruction. The Oakleaf Project

#	Category				?	?
1.	PERCENTAGE OF STUDENT BODY					
2.	PERCENTAGE OF SCHOOL TIME					
3.	ATTENDANCE	Optional	School Not Class	Class Not Sub-Group	Mandatory	
4.	MATERIALS FOR STUDY	Individual Choice	Individual Prescribed	Sub-Group Prescribed Or Discussed	Class/Grade Prescribed	
5.	METHOD OF STUDYING MATERIALS	Individual Choice	Individual Prescribed	Sub-Group Prescribed Or Discussed	Class/Grade Prescribed	
6.	PACE OF STUDY	Individual Choice	Individual Prescribed	Sub-Group Prescribed Or Discussed	Class/Grade Prescribed	
7.	ACTIVITY	Individual Choice	Individual Prescribed	Sub-Group Prescribed Or Discussed	Class/Grade Prescribed	
8.	DECISION-MAKING	Student (Permissive)	Student and Teacher (Responsive)	Teacher (Active)	Administrative Authority	
9.	TEACHING FOCUS	Values	Processes	Skill Concepts	Content	
10.	TEACHING FUNCTION	Teacher Available	Teacher Guides	Teacher Presents	Teacher Directs	
11.	TEACHING METHOD	Unspecified Discovery (Permissive)	Guided Discovery (Problem Solving)	Explanation and Discussion	Drill Exercise Repetition	
12.	ENVIRONMENT	Community	School	Classroom or Resource Area	Desk	
13.	TIME STRUCTURE	Non-Structured	Fluid	Structured Non-Structured	Structured	
14.	EVALUATION	Student Self-Evaluation	Broad Assessment	Quantity Of Work	Exam-Class Rank	
15.	PURPOSES OF PROGRAM	Continuous Development To Maturity	Adjustment	Understanding	Efficient Mastery	

Profile 4: Programmed Instruction (Linear)

#	Category				
1.	PERCENTAGE OF STUDENT BODY				
2.	PERCENTAGE OF SCHOOL TIME				
3.	ATTENDANCE	Optional	School Not Class	Class Not Sub-Group	Mandatory
4.	MATERIALS FOR STUDY	Individual Choice	Individual Prescribed	Sub-Group Prescribed Or Discussed	Class/Grade Prescribed
5.	METHOD OF STUDYING MATERIALS	Individual Choice	Individual Prescribed	Sub-Group Prescribed Or Discussed	Class/Grade Prescribed
6.	PACE OF STUDY	Individual Choice	Individual Prescribed	Sub-Group Prescribed Or Discussed	Class/Grade Prescribed
7.	ACTIVITY	Individual Choice	Individual Prescribed	Sub-Group Prescribed Or Discussed	Class/Grade Prescribed
8.	DECISION-MAKING	Student (Permissive)	Student and Teacher (Responsive)	Teacher (Active)	Administrative Authority
9.	TEACHING FOCUS	Values	Processes	Skill Concepts	Content
10.	TEACHING FUNCTION	Teacher Available	Teacher Guides	Teacher Presents	Teacher Directs
11.	TEACHING METHOD	Unspecified Discovery (Permissive)	Guided Discovery (Problem Solving)	Explanation and Discussion	Drill Exercise Repetition
12.	ENVIRONMENT	Community	School	Classroom or Resource Area	Desk
13.	TIME STRUCTURE	Non-Structured	Fluid	Structured Non-Structured	Structured
14.	EVALUATION	Student Self-Evaluation	Broad Assessment	Quantity Of Work	Exam-Class Rank
15.	PURPOSES OF PROGRAM	Continuous Development To Maturity	Adjustment	Understanding	Efficient Mastery

Profile 5: The Dalton Laboratory Plan

1. PERCENTAGE OF STUDENT BODY				
2. PERCENTAGE OF SCHOOL TIME				
3. ATTENDANCE	Optional	School Not Class	Class Not Sub-Group	Mandatory
4. MATERIALS FOR STUDY	Individual Choice	Individual Prescribed	Sub-Group Prescribed Or Discussed	Class/Grade Prescribed
5. METHOD OF STUDYING MATERIALS	Individual Choice	Individual Prescribed	Sub-Group Prescribed Or Discussed	Class/Grade Prescribed
6. PACE OF STUDY	Individual Choice	Individual Prescribed	Sub-Group Prescribed Or Discussed	Class/Grade Prescribed
7. ACTIVITY	Individual Choice	Individual Prescribed	Sub-Group Prescribed Or Discussed	Class/Grade Prescribed
8. DECISION-MAKING	Student (Permissive)	Student and Teacher (Responsive)	Teacher (Active)	Administrative Authority
9. TEACHING FOCUS	Values	Processes	Skill Concepts	Content
10. TEACHING FUNCTION	Teacher Available	Teacher Guides	Teacher Presents	Teacher Directs
11. TEACHING METHOD	Unspecified Discovery (Permissive)	Guided Discovery (Problem Solving)	Explanation and Discussion	Drill Exercise Repetition
12. ENVIRONMENT	Community	School	Classroom or Resource Area	Desk
13. TIME STRUCTURE	Non-Structured	Fluid	Structured Non-Structured	Structured
14. EVALUATION	Student Self-Evaluation	Broad Assessment	Quantity Of Work	Exam-Class Rank
15. PURPOSES OF PROGRAM	Continuous Development To Maturity	Adjustment	Understanding	Efficient Mastery

Profile 6: The Winnetka Plan

1.	PERCENTAGE OF STUDENT BODY	Optional	School Not Class	Class Not Sub-Group	Mandatory
2.	PERCENTAGE OF SCHOOL TIME				
3.	ATTENDANCE	Optional	School Not Class	Class Not Sub-Group	Mandatory
4.	MATERIALS FOR STUDY	Individual Choice	Individual Prescribed	Sub-Group Prescribed Or Discussed	Class/Grade Prescribed
5.	METHOD OF STUDYING MATERIALS	Individual Choice	Individual Prescribed	Sub-Group Prescribed Or Discussed	Class/Grade Prescribed
6.	PACE OF STUDY	Individual Choice	Individual Prescribed	Sub-Group Prescribed Or Discussed	Class/Grade Prescribed
7.	ACTIVITY	Individual Choice	Individual Prescribed	Sub-Group Prescribed Or Discussed	Class/Grade Prescribed
8.	DECISION-MAKING	Student (Permissive)	Student and Teacher (Responsive)	Teacher (Active)	Administrative Authority
9.	TEACHING FOCUS	Values	Processes	Skill Concepts	Content
10.	TEACHING FUNCTION	Teacher Available	Teacher Guides	Teacher Presents	Teacher Directs
11.	TEACHING METHOD	Unspecified Discovery (Permissive)	Guided Discovery (Problem Solving)	Explanation and Discussion	Drill Exercise Repetition
12.	ENVIRONMENT	Community	School	Classroom or Resource Area	Desk
13.	TIME STRUCTURE	Non-Structured	Fluid	Structured Non-Structured	Structured
14.	EVALUATION	Student Self-Evaluation	Broad Assessment	Quantity Of Work	Exam-Class Rank
15.	PURPOSES OF PROGRAM	Continuous Development To Maturity	Adjustment	Understanding	Efficient Mastery

Profile 7. An Independent Study Program: Abington

Not Clarified

#	Category				
1.	PERCENTAGE OF STUDENT BODY				
2.	PERCENTAGE OF SCHOOL TIME				
3.	ATTENDANCE	Optional	School Not Class	Class Not Sub-Group	Mandatory
4.	MATERIALS FOR STUDY	Individual Choice	Individual Prescribed	Sub-Group Prescribed Or Discussed	Class/Grade Prescribed
5.	METHOD OF STUDYING MATERIALS	Individual Choice	Individual Prescribed	Sub-Group Prescribed Or Discussed	Class/Grade Prescribed
6.	PACE OF STUDY	Individual Choice	Individual Prescribed	Sub-Group Prescribed Or Discussed	Class/Grade Prescribed
7.	ACTIVITY	Individual Choice	Individual Prescribed	Sub-Group Prescribed Or Discussed	Class/Grade Prescribed
8.	DECISION-MAKING	Student (Permissive)	Student and Teacher (Responsive)	Teacher (Active)	Administrative Authority
9.	TEACHING FOCUS	Values	Processes	Skill Concepts	Content
10.	TEACHING FUNCTION	Teacher Available	Teacher Guides	Teacher Presents	Teacher Directs
11.	TEACHING METHOD	Unspecified Discovery (Permissive	Guided Discovery (Problem Solving)	Explanation and Discussion	Drill Exercise Repetition
12.	ENVIRONMENT	Community	School	Classroom or Resource Area	Desk
13.	TIME STRUCTURE	Non-Structured	Fluid	Structured Non-Structured	Structured
14.	EVALUATION	Student Self-Evaluation	Broad Assessment	Quantity Of Work	Exam-Class Rank
15.	PURPOSES OF PROGRAM	Continuous Development To Maturity	Adjustment	Understanding	Efficient Mastery

Profile 8: Leicestershire Schools

	Category				
1.	PERCENTAGE OF STUDENT BODY				
2.	PERCENTAGE OF SCHOOL TIME				
3.	ATTENDANCE	Optional	School Not Class	Class Not Sub-Group	Mandatory
4.	MATERIALS FOR STUDY	Individual Choice	Individual Prescribed	Sub-Group Prescribed Or Discussed	Class/Grade Prescribed
5.	METHOD OF STUDYING MATERIALS	Individual Choice	Individual Prescribed	Sub-Group Prescribed Or Discussed	Class/Grade Prescribed
6.	PACE OF STUDY	Individual Choice	Individual Prescribed	Sub-Group Prescribed Or Discussed	Class/Grade Prescribed
7.	ACTIVITY	Individual Choice	Individual Prescribed	Sub-Group Prescribed Or Discussed	Class/Grade Prescribed
8.	DECISION-MAKING	Student (Permissive)	Student and Teacher (Responsive)	Teacher (Active)	Administrative Authority
9.	TEACHING FOCUS	Values	Processes	Skill Concepts	Content
10.	TEACHING FUNCTION	Teacher Available	Teacher Guides	Teacher Presents	Teacher Directs
11.	TEACHING METHOD	Unspecified Discovery (Permissive)	Guided Discovery (Problem Solving)	Explanation and Discussion	Drill Exercise Repetition
12.	ENVIRONMENT	Community	School	Classroom or Resource Area	Desk
13.	TIME STRUCTURE	Non-Structured	Fluid	Structured Non-Structured	Structured
14.	EVALUATION	Student Self-Evaluation	Broad Assessment	Quantity Of Work	Exam-Class Rank
15.	PURPOSES OF PROGRAM	Continuous Development To Maturity	Adjustment	Understanding	Efficient Mastery

Profile 9. Summerhill

1. PERCENTAGE OF STUDENT BODY				
2. PERCENTAGE OF SCHOOL TIME				
3. ATTENDANCE	Optional	School Not Class	Class Not Sub-Group	Mandatory
4. MATERIALS FOR STUDY	Individual Choice	Individual Prescribed	Sub-Group Prescribed Or Discussed	Class/Grade Prescribed
5. METHOD OF STUDYING MATERIALS	Individual Choice	Individual Prescribed	Sub-Group Prescribed Or Discussed	Class/Grade Prescribed
6. PACE OF STUDY	Individual Choice	Individual Prescribed	Sub-Group Prescribed Or Discussed	Class/Grade Prescribed
7. ACTIVITY	Individual Choice	Individual Prescribed	Sub-Group Prescribed Or Discussed	Class/Grade Prescribed
8. DECISION-MAKING	Student (Permissive)	Student and Teacher (Responsive)	Teacher (Active)	Administrative Authority
9. TEACHING FOCUS	Values	Processes	Skill Concepts	Content
10. TEACHING FUNCTION	Teacher Available	Teacher Guides	Teacher Presents	Teacher Directs
11. TEACHING METHOD	Unspecified Discovery (Permissive)	Guided Discovery (Problem Solving)	Explanation and Discussion	Drill Exercise Repetition
12. ENVIRONMENT	Community	School	Classroom or Resource Area	Desk
13. TIME STRUCTURE	Non-Structured	Fluid	Structured Non-Structured	Structured
14. EVALUATION	Student Self-Evaluation	Broad Assessment	Quantity Of Work	Exam-Class Rank
15. PURPOSES OF PROGRAM	Continuous Development To Maturity	Adjustment	Understanding	Efficient Mastery

Profile 10. Actual Performance (Broken line) Compared with Leicestershire Profile (Solid line)

SOURCES

Adams, John. *Modern Developments in Educational Practice.* New York: Harcourt, Brace, 1926.

Alexander, William M.; Hines, Vynce A.; and associates. *Independent Study in Secondary Schools.* New York: Holt, Rinehart and Winston, 1967.

Anderson, Robert H. *Teaching in a World of Change.* New York: Harcourt, Brace & World, 1966.

Beggs, David W., and Buffie, Edward G. (eds.). *Independent Study: Bold New Venture.* Bloomington: Indiana University Press, 1965.

Bishop, Lloyd K. "Independent Study." *The Clearing House,* Vol. XLII, No. 1 (September 1967), pp. 9–14.

Bloom, Benjamin S. (ed.). *Taxonomy of Educational Objectives: Handbook 1: Cognitive Domain.* New York: McKay, 1956.

Borton, Terry. "What Turns Kids On?" *Saturday Review,* April 15, 1967, pp. 72–74, 80.

71

Brown, Frank B. *The Non-Graded High School*. Englewood Cliffs, N.J.: Prentice-Hall, 1963.

Chall, Jeanne S. and others. *Learning to Read: The Great Debate*. New York: McGraw-Hill, 1967.

Children and their primary schools: A report of the Central Advisory Council for Education (England). Vol. 1. London: H.M.S.O., 1967.

A Climate for Individuality. Statement of the Joint Project on the Individual and the School. Washington, D.C.: American Association of School Administrators, 1965.

Clymer, T., and Kearney, N. C. "Curricular Instructional Provisions for Individual Differences." In N. B. Henry (ed.), *Individualizing Instruction*. Sixty-first Yearbook (Part 1) of the National Society for the Study of Education. Chicago: University of Chicago Press, 1962. Pp. 265–282.

Coleman, James, *et al. Equality of Educational Opportunity*. Washington, D.C.: U.S. Government Printing Office, 1966.

Coombs, Arthur W. "Fostering Self-Direction." *Educational Leadership,* Vol. XXIII (February 1966), pp. 373–376.

Cremin, Lawrence A. *The Transformation of the School*. New York: Vintage Books, 1961.

Crowder, Norman A. "Intrinsic Programming: Facts, Fallacies, and Future." In Robert T. Filep (ed.), *Prospectives in Programming*. New York: Macmillan, 1963.

Criuckshank, William M., and Johnson, G. Orville. *Education of Exceptional Children and Youth* (2nd ed.). Englewood Cliffs, N.J.: Prentice-Hall, 1967.

Cyphert, F. R. "Independent Study: The Dilemma." *Theory Into Practice,* Vol. V, No. 5 (1966), pp. 205–208.

De Cecco, John P. (ed.). *Educational Technology.* New York: Holt, Rinehart and Winston, 1964.

DeHaan, R. F., and Doll, R. C. "Individualization and Human Potential." In R. C. Doll (ed.), *Individualizing Instruction.* Washington, D.C.: Association for Supervision and Curriculum Development, 1964. Pp. 9–28.

Doll, E. "Preface." In J. Hellmuth (ed.), *Learning Disorders,* Vol. I. Seattle: Special Child Publications of the Sequin School, 1965. Pp. i–ii.

Doll, Ronald C. (ed.). *Individualizing Instruction.* Washington, D.C.: Association for Supervision and Curriculum Development, 1964.

Erikson, Erik H. (ed.). *The Challenge of Youth.* New York: Anchor Books, 1965.

————. *Childhood and Society.* New York: W. W. Norton, 1964.

Esbensen, Thorwald. *Working with Individualized Instruction.* Palo Alto: Fearon, 1968.

"The Everdale Place: A School Community." *This Magazine Is About Schools,* Vol. I, No. 3 (Winter 1967), pp. 77–106.

Featherstone, Joseph. "Schools for Children: What's Happening in British Classrooms." *The New Republic,* August 19, 1967, pp. 17–21. (a)

————. "How Children Learn." *The New Republic,* September 2, 1967, pp. 17–21. (b)

————. "Teaching Children to Think." *The New Republic,* September 9, 1967, pp. 15–19. (c)

Flanagan, John C. "Project Plan: Basic Assumptions, Implementation and Significance." A paper delivered at the American Educational Research Association Conference, Minneapolis, March 3, 1970.

Frazier, Alexander (ed.). *New Insights and the Curriculum*. Washington, D.C.: Association for Supervision and Curriculum Development, 1963.

Friedenberg, Edgar Z. *The Vanishing Adolescent*. New York: Dell Publishing Co., 1959.

Garner, Ronald A. "Independent Study in Secondary Schools." In *Curriculum Bulletin*, No. 281 (August 1967), published by School of Education, University of Oregon, Eugene, Oregon.

Gibbons, Maurice. "Systematic Development in Schooling." *The Journal of Education*, No. 16 (April 1970), pp. 32–43.

Glaser, Robert (ed.). *Teaching Machines and Programed Learning*, II. Washington, D.C.: National Education Association, 1965.

Glatthorn, A. A., and Ferderbar, J. E. "Independent Study—For *All* Students." *Phi Delta Kappan*, Vol. 47 (March 1966), pp. 379–382.

Gleason, Gerald T. (ed.). *The Theory and Nature of Independent Learning*. Scranton: International Textbook, 1967.

Goodlad, John I. "Classroom Organization." In Chester W. Harris (ed.), *Encyclopedia of Educational Research*. New York: Macmillan, 1960.

————, and Anderson, Robert H. *The Non-Graded Elementary School*. New York: Harcourt, Brace & World, 1959.

Goodman, Paul. *Compulsory Mis-Education, and the Community of Scholars.* New York: Random House (Vintage Books), 1966.

————. *Growing Up Absurd.* New York: Random House (Vintage Books), 1956.

Grannis, Joseph C. "Team Teaching and the Curriculum." In J. T. Shaplin and H. F. Olds, Jr. (eds.), *Team Teaching.* New York: Harper & Row, 1964. Pp. 123–167.

Guilford, J. P. *The Nature of Human Intelligence.* New York: McGraw Hill, 1967.

Harris, Chester W. (ed.). *Encyclopedia of Educational Research.* New York: Macmillan, 1960.

Hellmuth, Jerome (ed.). *Learning Disorders.* Vols. I and II. Seattle: Special Child Publications of the Sequin School, 1965.

Henry, Nelson B. (ed.). *The Dynamics of Instructional Groups.* Fifty-ninth Yearbook (Part 2) of the National Society for the Study of Education. Chicago: University of Chicago Press, 1960.

————. (ed.). *Individualizing Instruction.* Eighty-first Yearbook (Part 1) of the National Society for the Study of Education. Chicago: University Press, 1962.

Hess, Robert D., and Bear, Roberta Myer (eds.). *Early Education: Current Theory, Research and Action.* (Conference on Pre-school Education, Chicago, 1966). Chicago: Aldine, 1968.

Holland, James G. "Teaching Machines: An Application of Principles from the Laboratory." *Journal of the Experimental Analysis of Behavior,* Vol. III, No. 4 (October 1960), pp. 275–287.

Holt, John. *How Children Fail.* New York: Dell (Delta Books), 1964.

————. *How Children Learn.* New York: Pitman, 1967.

Hull, W. P. "Leicestershire Revisited." A mimeographed report, August 1964.

Jackson, Philip W. "The Teacher and the Machine." Paper prepared for the Committee for Economic Development, September 1966.

Johnson, Olive. "As a cool school, there's no place like Knowplace." *MacLean's Magazine,* Vol. 80 (December 1967), p. 5.

Jourard, S. "Fascination: A Phenomenological Perspective on Independent Learning." In G. T. Gleason (ed.), *The Theory and Nature of Independent Learning.* Scranton: International Textbook, 1967. Pp. 79–101.

Kallet, Tony. "Two Classrooms." *This Magazine Is About Schools,* Vol. I, No. 1 (Winter 1966), pp. 45–49.

Kapfer, Philip G. "An Instructional Management Strategy for Individualized Learning." *Phi Delta Kappan,* Vol. 49 (January 1968), pp. 260–263.

Kohn, Sherwood D. *Profiles of Significant Schools: Three High Schools Revisited: Andrews, McPherson and Nova.* New York: Report from Educational Facilities Laboratories, July 1967.

Kozol, Jonathan. "A Junior High That's Like a College." *The New York Times Magazine,* October 29, 1967, pp. 24–32, 121–132.

Krathwohl, David R., *et al. Taxonomy of Educational Objectives: Handbook 2: Affective Domain.* New York: McKay, 1964.

Montessori, Maria. *The Montessori Method.* (Anne E. George, trans.) New York: Schocken, 1964.

Neill, A. S. *Summerhill.* New York: Hart Publishing Co., 1960.

New Approaches to Individualizing Instruction. Princeton: Educational Testing Service, 1965.

Newmann, Fred M., and Oliver, Donald W. "Education and Community." *Harvard Educational Review,* Vol. XXXI, No. 1 (Winter 1967), pp. 61–106.

Noffsinger, John S. *Correspondence Schools, Lyceums, Chautaquas.* New York: Macmillan, 1926.

Olson, Willard. "Seeking, Self-selection and Pacing in the Use of Books." *The Packet.* Boston: Heath, 1952.

Outward Bound Schools. Andover: Outward Bound, [n.d.].

Parker, Don H. *Schooling for Individual Excellence.* New York: Nelson, 1963.

Parker, J. Cecil, and Rubin, Louis J. *Process as Content.* Chicago: Rand McNally, 1966.

Parkhurst, Helen. *Education on the Dalton Plan.* New York: Dutton, 1922.

Pearse, Benjamin H. "The Postman is the Proctor." *American Education,* Vol. III (February 1967), pp. 10–12.

Peter, Lawrence J. *Prescriptive Teaching.* New York: McGraw-Hill, 1965.

Pines, Maya. *Revolution in Learning.* New York: Harper & Row, 1967.

Polos, N. C. "Tutorial Adapted for the High School." *The Clearing House,* Vol. XL (March 1966), pp. 404–405.

"The Project for Individually Prescribed Instruction (Oakleaf Project)." Mimeographed article [University of Pittsburgh] [n.d.].

Rambusch, Nancy McCormick. *Learning How to Learn: An American Approach to Montessori.* Baltimore: Helicon Press, 1962.

Richardson, Elwyn S. *In the Early World.* Wellington, N.Z.: New Zealand Council of Educational Research, 1964.

Rogers, Carl R. *Client-Centered Therapy.* Boston: Houghton Mifflin, 1951.

————. *On Becoming a Person.* Boston: Houghton Mifflin, 1961.

————. *Freedom to Learn.* Columbus: Merrill, 1969.

Schlesinger, Joy. "Leicestershire Report: The Classroom Environment." Mimeographed [Educational Services, Inc.] [n.d.].

Search, Preston. "The Pueblo Plan of Individual Teaching." *Educational Review,* Vol. VIII (June 1894), pp. 84–85.

Shane, H. G. "The School and Individual Differences." In N. B. Henry (ed.), *Individualizing Instruction.* Sixty-first Yearbook (Part 1) of the National Society for the Study of Education. Chicago: University of Chicago Press, 1962. Pp. 44–61.

Shaplin, Judson T., and Olds, Henry F., Jr. (eds.). *Team Teaching.* New York: Harper & Row, 1964.

Skinner, B. F. "Teaching Machines." *Scientific American,* Vol. 205 (November 1961), pp. 90–102.

Spitzer, Lillian K. *A Selected Bibliography on Individualizing Instruction.* Mimeographed. I.D.E.A., 1968.

Stauffer, Russell. "Individualized and Group Type Directed Reading Instruction." *Elementary English,* Vol. XXXVII (October 1960), pp. 375–382.

Stephens, J. M. *The Process of Schooling.* New York: Holt, Rinehart & Winston, 1967.

Taba, Hilda. *Curriculum Development: Theory and Practice.* New York: Harcourt, Brace & World, 1962.

Thelen, Herbert A. *Dynamics of Groups at Work.* Chicago: The University of Chicago Press (Phoenix Edition), 1963.

Thomas, R. Murray, and Thomas, Shirley M. *Individual Differences in the Classroom.* New York: McKay, 1965.

Tirrell, John E. "Total (!!) Independent Study at Oakland." *Junior College Journal,* Vol. XXXVI (April 1966), pp. 21–23.

Trump, J. Lloyd, and Baynam, Dorsey. *Focus on Change: Guide to Better Schools.* New York: Rand McNally, 1961.

Tyler, Leona E. *The Psychology of Human Differences.* New York: Appleton-Century-Crofts, 1956.

Tyler, Ralph W. *Basic Principles of Curriculum and Instruction.* Chicago: University of Chicago Press, 1950.

Wallach, M. A., and Kogan, N. *Modes of Thinking in Young Children.* New York: Holt, 1965.

Washburne, Carleton. *A Living Philosophy of Education.* New York: Day, 1940.

———, and Marland, Sidney P., Jr. *Winnetka: The History and Significance of an Educational Experiment.* Englewood Cliffs, N.J.: Prentice-Hall, 1963.

Watertown and the Education of Its Children. Cambridge: The Center for Field Studies, Harvard Graduate School of Education, 1967.

Westby-Gibson, Dorothy. *Grouping Students for Improved Instruction.* Englewood Cliffs, N.J.: Prentice-Hall, 1966.

Whitmire, Janet. "The Independent Study Program at Melbourne High." *Phi Delta Kappan,* Vol. XLVII (September 1965), pp. 43–47.

Wilhelms, F. T. "The Curriculum and Individual Differences." In N. B. Henry (ed.), *Individualizing Instruction.* Sixty-first Yearbook (Part 1) of the National Society for the Study of Education. Chicago: University of Chicago Press, 1962. Pp. 62–74.

Wolfson, Bernice J. "Individualizing Instruction." *National Education Association Journal,* Vol. LV (November 1966), pp. 31–33.

Yeomans, Edward. *Education for Initiative and Responsibility.* Boston: National Association of Independent Schools, 1967.